Whispers of the Soul

A Collection of Heartfelt Poems

PAUL KNOX

Email: Jundi.writes@gmail.com
ISBN: 9798218355890
Paul Knox
P.O. Box 11862
Philadelphia, PA 19128

About the Book

"***Whispers of the Soul***" is a compelling collection of heartfelt poems that eloquently captures the myriad emotions of human existence. Delving deep into the realms of love, loss, joy, and self-discovery, these poetic verses resonate with readers from all walks of life.

This enchanting anthology takes readers on a thought-provoking journey through life's ups and downs, aspiring to celebrate the beauty of the human experience. Each poem tells a story of its own, painted with vivid imagery and lyrical language, allowing readers to connect intimately with the emotions and experiences expressed within its pages.

You will be captivated by the exploration of love, its ecstasy, and heartache, as the poems delve into the complexities of relationships, unrequited love, and the bittersweet moments that make love the most profound of emotions. The verses breathe life into the joys of self-discovery, addressing the unearthing of one's true identity, embracing vulnerability, and finding strength within.

The somber notes of loss and grief are depicted with hauntingly beautiful poetry, offering solace to those who have endured difficult goodbyes and reminding readers of the resilience of the human spirit. These poems touch upon the themes of healing, resilience, and the transformative power of embracing pain as a catalyst for growth.

"***Whispers of the Soul***" is an inspiring collection that invites readers to embrace their own emotions and reflect on the profundity of the human experience. It is a testament to the power of words to heal, awaken, and unite us, reminding us all that we are not alone in our joys and sorrows.

This anthology is the perfect companion for those seeking solace and nourishment for the soul, offering respite from the fast-paced world and inviting readers to pause, reflect, and connect with their own innermost emotions.

Editor's Comment

Whispers of the Soul is like a well-brewed wine. It is a wonderful literary piece artistically woven. The message therein pierces directly into the sense organs, creating an indelible positive image. The subject matter, themes, diction, rhythm and rhyme scheme, and the poet's lavish use of poetic devices, further make the work a great literary work. In these poems, there is a reflection of wit and wisdom, and the creative expertise of not just a mere writer but of an experienced and gifted poet whose voice resonates, soothes, and breathes life into a dying soul. The poems are didactic. Sincerely speaking, these poems are among the best poems I have ever read. I recommend this anthology to all and sundry. Kudos to this great poet of our time, Jundi.

Dedication

To my hero, my beacon of strength, my guiding light, my loving mother - Shelly D. Knox-Blocker.

Your love has been my sanctuary, your wisdom my guide, your resilience my inspiration. From you, I learned the power of words, the beauty of empathy, and the strength of vulnerability. I have watched you weave tales of life, love, and loss into a tapestry of human emotion in your book "*Silent Tears I've Cried*".

This book is dedicated to you - not just for the love you've showered upon me, but for the courage you've displayed in sharing your journey with the world. Your words have touched the hearts of many, reminding us all of our shared humanity.

You've shown us that even in our silent tears, we are not alone. Your strength in adversity, your grace under pressure, and your unyielding faith have painted a portrait of a warrior, a survivor, a hero.

You are more than just my mother; you are a beacon of hope to countless hearts. Through your words and your life, you've taught us that even in the darkest nights, dawn is but a heartbeat away.

Thank you, Mom, for every lesson taught, every tear wiped, and every dream nurtured. This book is a testament to your indomitable spirit, your unwavering love, and your invaluable wisdom.

With all my love and admiration,"T"

Table of Contents

Dear Father,

A title worn so thin,
39 years, where have you been?
Birthdays passed, no cards, no call,
Only echoes in an empty hall.

Candles lit and wishes made,
In your shadow, joy would fade.
Promises given, yet never kept,
In their silence, I have wept.

For every scrape, for every fall,
I searched for you, but you'd withdrawn.
Absent whispers, absent cheers,
My milestones are marked by absent years.
39 times the cake was cut,
Inside my heart, the door was shut.
Yearning for a father's touch,
Craving for what I missed so much.

Yet in this void, this hollow space,
I found strength, I found grace.
Your absence was my greatest trial,
Yet from the ashes, I did rise.

Now I stand, a man grown tall,
Out of the shadow, breaking the wall.
In your absence, I found my worth,
A journey started at my birth.

Dear Father, who owes me so,
I've let go of the hurt, the woe.
39 candles burned to the ground,
In their ashes, forgiveness was found.

The debt is cleared, we're on a new page,
A lighter heart, free of rage.
I've grown in ways you'll never see,
Your absence was a gift to me.

So, Dear Father, wherever you roam,
Know your son has found his home.
39 years, 39 strides,
On my own, with pride, I rise.

To my Loving Soulmate

In the vast expanse of time, my soulmate awaits,
A connection so profound, that destiny orchestrates.
Across the tapestry of life, our paths intertwine,
Bound by a divine love, forever entwined.

In the quiet spaces of my heart, your presence I feel,
An ethereal flame, a connection so real.
Unseen, yet palpable, this cosmic embrace,
A bond that transcends time and space.

Through the corridors of fate, we approach closer,
With each passing moment, the allure grows bolder.
In the whispers of the wind, I hear your name,
In the depths of my dreams, our souls are aflame.

We may have yet to cross paths in this world,
But destiny, dear soulmate, won't be unfurled.
For in each beat of the heart, and breath I take,
I know that our bond will never break.

So, to you, my dear soulmate, wherever you may be,
Know that my love for you extends eternally.
In this vast existence, we'll find our way,
For in the tapestry of love, we were meant to stay.

Until the day our paths intertwine,
I'll hold you in my heart, my love divine.
For time may be fleeting, but love never dies,
And in each passing moment, our connection will rise.

So, dear soulmate, wherever you may dwell,
Know that my love for you forever will swell.
Until the day we finally meet,
I'll wait patiently, my heart at your feet.

For our souls are destined to unite,
In a love that burns eternally bright.
And until that moment, I'll simply be,
Dreaming of the day I'll call you my soulmate, you see.

My Fellow Veterans

Dear Fellow Veterans of the United States Armed Services, especially the Paratroopers,

I hope this letter finds you in good health and spirits.
I wanted to take a moment to reach out and express my love and deep appreciation for each and every one of you.
Our shared experiences, sacrifices, and the bonds we formed during our service are truly special.

First and foremost, I want you all to know that I love you.
Our time together, whether on the front lines or behind the scenes, has created an unbreakable connection that extends beyond our military service.
We have faced challenges together, relied on each other, and formed lifelong friendships that transcend time and distance.

I also want to emphasize that if there is ever a moment when I can be of service to any of you, please do not hesitate to reach out.
Whether it's a listening ear, support during tough times, or assistance with any challenges you may be facing, I am here for you.
We are a family, and supporting one another is what we do best.

Additionally, I extend an open invitation for my brothers and sisters to check on me from time to time.
Let us continue to uplift one another, sharing our joys and burdens, as we navigate through life beyond the military.

In closing, know that my love and support for each and every one of you is unwavering. Our time in service has shaped us into the resilient individuals we are today, and I am proud to call you my fellow veterans. May we always find strength and solace in our shared experiences.

With all my love and gratitude,

Jundi

Dear Enemies,

To all my foes, my dearest foes,
I pen this verse, a quiet prose.
For though you may wish ill on me,
I'll rise above, forever free.

In shadows dark, you plot and scheme,
Your jealousy is a constant theme.
But now, I stand with my head held high,
Your malice fails to make me sigh.

For every word you twist and turn,
I find strength, the fire within burns.
You see, dear foes, your spiteful art,
Can never break this steadfast heart.

I weave my dreams, undeterred,
No hate or scorn has ever blurred,
The path I tread, with purpose bright,
I'll chase my goals, and exude my light.

Your envy fuels the daggers thrown,
But still, I stand, unyielding stone.
For every stumble, I'll rise again,
With determination, and no disdain.

So, thank you, foes, for the fight,
Your presence fuels my inner might.
As I move forward, head held high,
Your enmity will pass me by.

For, in the end, it's clear to see,
Your hatred only strengthens me.
I'll soar above this petty game,
And leave you behind, in envy's shame.

So, here's my message, loud and clear,
May peace be found, to end the fear.
For while you seek to bring me low,
I'll rise above and brighter glow.

A letter to my sister

Oh, dear sister, as the days go by,I cannot help but let out a sigh,
For you, my sibling, are a treasure so rare,
In your presence, life is beyond compare.

Through thick and thin, we have walked together,
From childhood mischief to stormy weather,
You've always been there, my guiding light,
A constant source of love and delight.

Your laughter sparkles like a gentle breeze,
In your smile, the world finds ease,
Your heart, so pure and filled with grace,
Lights up every corner of this earthly space.

In moments of sadness, you offer your hand,
Comforting words, you always understand,
You listen without judgment, my confidante true,
With you, sister, there's nothing I can't pursue.

Through each season, we've embraced change,
Our bond grew stronger and never estranged,
And though distance may keep us apart,
You reside forever in the depths of my heart.

So, on this day, as the years unfold,
I express my love, unbreakable and bold, My sister, my friend, my soul's companion,
May our connection continue to deepen and strengthen.

For you are the stars that light up my night,
With you by my side, life feels just right,
Forever grateful for the love we've known,
Sister dear, may our bond forever be sown.

Slumlords

Dear landlord, I pen this verse to thee,
With hopes that you will truly see,
The grievances that weigh upon my heart,
And it's time for us to have a fresh start.

The rent we pay is a hefty fee,
Yet the value we receive is hard to see,
Every month, it cuts a little deeper,
Leaving us scrambling for pennies to keep.

The living conditions leave much to desire,Moldy walls
and leaking pipes conspire,
To ruin our comfort and peace of mind,
As we struggle to make it through each night.

When bugs invade, we feel invaded,
Their presence makes us feel degraded,
No peaceful rest, no sanctuary we find,
In the home, we thought we had left behind.

We pay our dues, we honor our part,
But it's time for change, for a fresh start,
Please understand our plea for betterment,
To alter the course of our predicament.

Reduce the rent, bring some solace nearby,
And address the issues that we hold dear,
Create a haven we can proudly call home,
A place where happiness can freely roam.

We seek a fair compromise, a middle ground,
Where burdens are shared and solutions found,Let's
foster a true landlord-tenant bond,
And together, build a place where we're truly found.

Dear landlord, our words may seem harsh,
But it's the only way to ignite the spark,
For change to happen, for improvement to show,
So we can live in the home we've come to know.

We hope you hear this plea, with open ears,
And recognize the weight of our fears,
For it's in this unity, that we can find a way,
To make this house a home, day by day.
Sincerely, your tenants who long for better,
In hope that you'll receive this heartfelt letter.

Kino

In the darkest hours, where shadows dwell,
Where confinement grips, and time seems to swell,
I write these words, dear friend, to ignite your soul,
To remind you of the strength that makes you whole.

Though the walls may hold you, and freedom feels far,
Within your spirit, burns a shining star,
A beacon of hope, a guiding light,
That will lead you through the longest night.

In this chapter of life, where struggles persist,
Remember, my friend, you were not meant to resist,
For within you lie a resilience so grand,
A strength that can weather any demand.

Through the days that drag and the nights that weigh,
Know that brighter horizons are not far away,
For time is a traveler, ever moving on,
Soon, my friend, this pain will be gone.

Though the present may seem like an endless strife,
Hold on tight to the memories of a free life,
For soon, the shackles will break, and you will be free,
To embrace a future where your dreams can roam free.

In the depths of your being, find the fire within,
The flame of courage that will help you begin,
To rise above the trials, the doubt, and the pain,
And to envision a future where freedom will reign.

Though the road may be rocky, the journey long,
Believe in yourself, and remain steadfast and strong,
For prison walls may hold your body still,
But they cannot cage the strength of your will.

So, my friend, hold your head high, don't despair,
For hope is a force that will always be there,
Soon, the memories of this time will fade,
As you step into a world where freedom is laid.

Prison may be a chapter in your life's story,
But it does not define your ultimate glory,
Remember, my friend, you have the power to change,
To rise above this darkness, to embrace the exchange.

So be brave, be resilient, and hold on tight,
For soon, my friend, you'll bask in the light,
Home will be waiting, with open arms wide,
And prison, a distant memory, left behind.

Chess-mate: To My Chess Opponent

Oh, a formidable opponent of mine,
Together in this battle, we intertwine,
With strategic moves upon the board,
Our minds embarked on a quest untoward.

A dance of intellect, a battle of wits,
In this game of chess, where honor submits,
Each moves a step, each piece a pawn,
We stand on a battlefield at dawn.

Oh knight, oh rook, oh bishop so wise,
With you, I learn to see beyond the disguise,
The intricacies hidden within the tides,
Of this ancient game where reason abides.

Your steady gaze, unwavering and sure,
Speaks of the knowledge you hold pure,
With each move, you challenge my might,
Forcing me to think, to question, to fight.

But fear not, my worthy adversary,
For it is through you I gain clarity,
For every pawn fallen, every piece took,
Teaches me the essence of the game, by the book.

And as our minds tango to the game's score,
I learn the secrets, forever wanting more,
The beauty lies not in victory, but in the dance,
In the harmony of choices, in this cosmic trance.

So, here's to you, my worthy foe,
Together we grow, together we know,
That in this ancient game, through every setback,
We find solace and mutual respect.

For it is in your challenges, that I thrive,
And it is through your wisdom, that I survive,
So let us cherish every move, every checkmate,
For it is through you, that I celebrate.

Oh formidable opponent, unmatched and pure,
Let us continue this game, let us endure,
For in this battle of minds, we both excel,
And as adversaries, we eternally dwell.

So here's to you, my chess companion,
In this game, we find our union,
Through the checkered board, we find delight,
In this perpetual dance, we unite.

Hey Boss!

Dear employer, I hope you'll hear,
These humble words that burden bear.
Though loyal I have been, it's clear,
Low pay and extra work foist nearby.

With hands that toil and spirits fade,
We strive to meet the tasks cascade.
But when the moon embraces night,
Toiling souls seek a fairer light.

In the quiet corners of our mind,
Resides a whisper, stark and kind.
A plea for equity, we beseech,
A reward that meets our labor's reach.

For every hour we give our all,
For every challenge, big or small,
Let appreciation gently flow,
And wages fair, we do bestow.

For in this realm of labor's art,
The value of each role takes part.
To build a prosperous enterprise,
Reward our efforts, we emphasize.

So, hear my plea, dear employer dear,
We seek a joyful atmosphere.
Fair compensation, that's just and right,
Will lead to harmony, day and night.

Together we can reach the sky,
With unity, our dreams are held high.
Let gratitude unite us strong,
In purpose, contentment, and make us belong.

For if we work as a team in kind,
A thriving future we will find.
So, employer dear, please take heed,
To these words of camaraderie and need.

With hope, we wait for your reply,
A future bright, where birds will fly.
Where low pay and extra work will cease,
And harmony will bring us peace.

My Dearest Children

To my beloved children, so dear and sweet,
These words I write, with love's gentle heartbeat,
I want you to know, my darlings so true,
That I love you, I miss you, and I'm sorry too.

Life's twists and turns, they've kept us apart,
But know, my loves, you're always in my heart,
Though circumstance intervened, causing this divide,
My love for you remains, a constant by your side.

I long to hold you close, to wipe away your tears,
To chase away your fears and calm your little fears,
But circumstances beyond our control, they prevail,
And for that, my angels, I deeply lament and bewail.

Please understand, my precious children so fair,
That my absence does not mean I do not care,
I yearn for the moments we could have shared,
But life's complexities have left us impaired.

I'm sorry for the moments I couldn't be there,
For the laughter, the joys, and the love we couldn't share,
But my love for you is unwavering and true,
And it will carry us through, no matter what we go through.

Hold on to the memories we've created before,
The love, the warmth, the joy at the core,
Know that I cherish each precious moment we've had,
And those memories will always make my heart glad.

Though I cannot be there physically, my loves,
Know that my spirit surrounds you like gentle doves,
I send you my love on the whispers of the wind,
Hoping you feel it deep within.

I love you, my children, with all of my being,
And though circumstances may be unyielding,
Please remember that love knows no bounds,
And in my heart, your love forever resounds.

So, my darlings, please hold on tight,
Keep your spirits strong, your hearts alight,
For the day may come when we'll reunite,
And the love we share will shine ever so bright.
With all my love and deepest apologies,
Your forever devoted parent.

A Warrior's Fight

In the darkness, where the demons' dwell,
A soldier walks, his soul a cell,
Haunted by battles fought and lost,
By burdens carried, at a heavy cost.

A heart so weary, spirit worn,
Depression's veil, forever torn,
Within his mind, a raging storm,
A wounded soul, in battle born.

The weight of sorrow, hard to bear,
Thoughts of suicide whispered in despair,
But amidst the darkness, a flicker of light,
A beacon of hope, shining so bright.

For even in the depths, strength can be found,
In camaraderie, in love, profound,
His brothers and sisters, standing tall,
Together they rise, never to fall.

Through tears and pain, they lend support,
A lifeline held, a bridge to escort,
Reaching out, their hands embrace,
Offering solace, in their warm embrace.

And in the silence of his darkest night,
A glimmer of hope, shining so bright,
For he is not alone, in this fight,
A soldier, finding strength, against the blight.

So let us stand, united as one,
In helping hands, the battles won,
For the burdens we carry, and the pain we share,
Can be lightened, when we truly care.

In the midst of despair, hope shall arise,
And the soldier shall soar, with newfound skies,
With love and support, his heart shall heal, From the
depths of despair, he shall reveal.

Tree of Life

In the heart of nature's embrace, there stands tall,
A gentle sentinel, the tree, for all to behold.
Its branches reaching out like arms, so wide,
Inviting souls to rest and confide.

Through seasons' passages, it remains steadfast,
A testament to resilience, a message that lasts.
In spring's awakening, it blossoms with grace,
An ode to new beginnings, a reflection of faith.

As summer's sun casts its golden rays,
The tree provides shelter from the scorching blaze.
Like a guardian of solace, it stands so strong,
Welcoming all creatures, where they belong.

When autumn arrives, colors paint its crown,
A kaleidoscope of orange, red, and brown.
A gentle reminder that change is nature's song,
Releasing what's no longer needed, moving along.

Beneath its boughs, whispers of wisdom abide,
The tree holds stories etched deep inside.
Its roots delve into the secrets of the earth,
Teaching us to find strength in our own birth.

In winter's frosty grip, it embraces the cold,
A resilient survivor, courageous and bold.
Bare branches reach towards the sky,
This a reminder to remain hopeful, and aim high.

Oh, tree of life, your beauty inspires,
Igniting passions and fulfilling desires.
A symbol of unity, growth, and grace,
A testament to the sacredness of this space.

So let us learn from this splendid tree,
To weather storms and set our spirits free.
In every season, in every form, it may be,
May we find strength and inspiration, just as the tree.

When the Chaplain Wants to Talk

In the depths of despair, confined and alone, In the
shadows of regrets, my spirit is thrown,
But even through bars, hope gently finds a way,
To mend broken hearts, to brighten the darkest day.

In this Philadelphia prison, where time stands still,I
search for solace, let positivity refill,
For I've lost precious souls, dear to my core,
Yet within these cold walls, their love forevermore.

Gone are the days of laughter and embrace,
Yet memories embrace me, like warmth's sweet grace,
They dance in my dreams, paint colors in my mind,
Their spirits surround me, in the darkest of times.

In this prison's silence, my heart finds release,
As the words on my paper, provide a much-needed
peace,
I reach beyond the bars, with ink-stained fingertips,
To share my story, to heal, to find friendship's grips.

Though I lay my head on a cold, iron bed,
My dreams soar freely, where sorrow is spread,
For even in this darkness, a light from within,
A ray of resilience, where possibilities begin.

Through these prison bars, my voice shall find grace,
To enlighten the lost, to inspire the displaced,
Through poetry's beauty, hope's song will arise,

Charting a path towards freedom in these wandering eyes.

For my loved ones departed, never far away,
Their spirits shine brightly, in my thoughts they stay,
Their absence may hurt, in these walls I reside,
But I carry their strength, in each tear that I hide.

So take solace, my friends, in the power of the pen, In the humblest ink drops, the strongest wings begin,
In this Philadelphia prison, where dreams can be reclaimed,
I rise above, I persevere, and I redefine my name.

Silent Echoes

From the depths of a heart that's known despair,
To another who feels life isn't fair,
I pen these words, sincere and true,
From one lonely soul to another like you.

In the abyss of gloom where we both reside,
Platonic friendship has been our guide.
Not lovers, not kin, but something deep,
A connection that soothes us in our sleep.

In the silence of suffering, we found each other,
Not bound by romance, but a bond like no other.
In the echo of our laughter, in our silent cries,
We found solace, under the same skies.

When the world around us seems false and jaded,
In our friendship, we find comfort unabated.
We share our fears, our hopes, our dreams,
In the gentle flow of life's unseen streams.

Through the veil of tears and the shadow of sorrow,
In our companionship, we find tomorrow.
A beacon of hope in the darkest night,
In each other, we find the strength to fight.

So, dear friend, when you feel lost and alone, you
Remember our bond, remember the strength you've
shown.
In the depths of despair, when all seems askew,
Remember, I'm fighting this battle with you.

When the fog of depression clouds your view,
Remember, my friend, I too am walking through.
In this dance of darkness, through each twist and bend,
Remember, you're not alone, you have a friend.

No Love Lost

To my dear ex-lovers, a heartfelt ode,
A chapter closed, but memories still owed.
Though paths diverged, and love's flame grew dim, I
cherish the moments shared, like a precious hymn.

With you, I tasted love's exquisite highs,Felt passions
stirring, painting the skies. Each of you brought a
unique melody, In the symphony of my romantic
reverie.

To the first, who ignited love's grand fire,You taught
me vulnerability and desire.
We danced through nights, dreaming of forever,
But fate intervened, and our paths were severed.

To the second, who taught me strength and grace,
You pushed me forward, finding my own space.
Through storms we weathered, hearts intertwining,
Yet we drifted apart, lost in the vast expanse of timing.

To the third, who showed me love's fragility,A brief
encounter, filled with intensity.
Our souls collided, but we couldn't sustain,
Leaving behind an echo of beauty and pain.
To the fourth, who brought laughter and light,

We reveled in moments, free from the night. But as
seasons changed, our love lost its way,Like fading
embers, extinguished in the gray

To the fifth, who healed wounds, showed me hope,
You offered solace on love's tightrope.
But as we grew closer, fears took their toll,
And love's refrain muted a story left untold.

To each of you, I offer gratitude,
For the lessons learned, in love's interlude.
Though paths diverged, and hearts turned away,
You colored my existence, in shades of yesterday.

So here's to the past, and what we once shared,
The trials of love, and the joy we dared.
May life bring you happiness, wherever you roam,
And may we remember our time, with fondness, not alone.

Nana

In memories cherished, a love so dear,
We gather today, with hearts sincere.
For Nana, who left us eighteen years ago, A
remembrance to honor, our love to show.

Her smile was like sunshine, a warmth so rare,
Her laughter was contagious, filling the air.
Her love was unconditional, a guiding light,Nana made
everything feel just right.

Though time has passed, her spirit remains,In the gentle
breeze, soft as summer rains.
Her love surrounds us, like a
comforting embrace,A presence
felt in every cherished place.

Through stories and photos, we reminisce,
Each memory becomes a treasured and timeless bliss.
Her love and wisdom, forever imprinted,
A legacy strong, never to be forgotten.

The lessons she taught, profound and deep,In our
hearts, her words forever keep.
Her kindness and compassion, a shining example,A
guiding star, in the darkest of nights ample.

Oh, Nana, we miss you with each passing day,
But in our hearts, your love will forever stay.
As we gather to remember and honor your name,

Know that you're loved, our eternal flame.

So let this poem be a tribute to you,
Nana, our guiding light, so pure and true.
In heaven's embrace, may you peacefully rest,

Knowing you're loved, eternally blessed.

Cosmic Mail

Oh Universe, you vast expanse of wonder,
A cosmic spectacle, where stars are born and sunder.
Invisible threads of gravity, your silent song, Holding
together, the weak and the strong.

Galaxies spin in your endless night,
Each a beacon, radiating celestial light,Planets and
moons in a cosmic dance,
In your infinite theatre, where comets prance.

Mystery cloaked in your dark matter veil, A cosmic
ocean, where humans set sail. Through telescopes, your
secrets we glean,Yet, so much remains unseen.

Your cosmic symphony in silent play,
From the fiery birth of stars to their final decay.Black
holes, your enigmatic heart,
Where space and time tear apart.
Your timescale, oh so vast and wide, A billion years, in
your graceful stride.
From the cosmic dawn to the distant future,
You unfold, in an endless adventure.

Universe, oh Universe, so profound and deep,
In your cosmic ocean, secrets you keep.
Humans, we are, on a pale blue dot,
In your grandeur, our troubles, are a mere afterthought.

Through your lens, we understand,
Our tiny place, in this cosmic sand.
Universe, oh Universe, in you we immerse,In awe and wonder, we pen this verse.

Betrayal Comes From Trust

Betrayal comes from trust, a bitter sting,
From hearts once filled with sweet echoing.
A dance of shadows in the twilight's gleam,An
agonizing twist in the love's soft dream.

Trust, sincere as a child's smile, so pure,
Becomes a puppet in the hands of allure.
Betrayal, the serpent lurking in the grass,
Strikes when hearts are vulnerable, alas.

Once upon a time, in the realm of trust,
Two souls entwined, in love robust.
Betrayal crept in, like a thief in the night,
Eclipsing their love, dimming the light.

Betrayal, the phantom, the heart's deceit,Turns trust into
a wound, bitter and deep.A stab in the back, a whisper of
lies,

A painful echo in the heart's silent cries.

The trust we give is a precious gift,To hold, to cherish,
not to lift.
Yet, when the veil of
love is torn, Betrayal
is born, leaving hearts
forlorn.

Can love survive the storm of deceit?
Can trust be rebuilt from the ruins of defeat?Bitter the
taste of the traitor's kiss,

In the dance of love, nothing hurts like this.

For betrayal is a wound that time may not heal,A
poison arrow, a pain too real.
From trust to treachery, a path so cruel, A game of
hearts, where fools often rule.

In the labyrinth of love, trust holds the key,

A beacon of hope for you and me.
Yet, beware of betrayal's venomous rust,
For it is born, where once lived trust.

Betrayal comes from trust, a warning to heed,
A lesson learned from love's bitter seed.
In the silent battles of heart and mind,
Trust carefully, for betrayal lurks behind.

My friend

In the realm of friendship, strong and true,I dedicate these words to you.
A poem, woven with love and care,
To remind you, my dear friend, that I'm always there.

Through the highs and lows we've shared,
In moments of joy and times of despair,
You've been a guiding light, a shining star,
A constant presence, no matter how far.

When laughter fills the air, you're by my side,
With every joke and silly smile, you provide.
Your humor brings comfort, like a warm embrace,
And my journey with you is a joy-filled race.

In times of sorrow, you lend an ear,
With empathy and kindness, your support is clear.
Your words of wisdom, like sunrays on my soul,
Help heal the wounds and make me whole.

Your friendship is an anchor, keeping me grounded,
In a world that sometimes feels confounded.
Through thick and thin, we've weathered the storm,
And our bond, unbreakable, takes a beautiful form.

So here's to you, my dearest friend,
May our friendship never know an end.
Thank you for being my rock, my confidant,
For being the one I can always count on.

In this world, so vast and wide,
You are the treasure by my side.
A friendship like ours deserves a grand cheer,For you,
my friend, I hold so dear.

End the Violence

In the vibrant streets of Philadelphia's land,
Where dreams take flight and futures are planned,
We gather today, with hearts ablaze,
To mend the path where violence lays.

Oh, fearless youth, the future's pride,
Let not your dreams in violence subside,
For deep within your souls reside,
The power to heal, for love, is your guide.

In tumultuous times, we find solace here,
To halt the anguish, to quell the fear,
United we stand, hand in hand,
To transform this city into a promised land.

Oh, children of hope, let your voices soar,
Break the chains of violence that bind us, and more,
For beneath the sorrow, lies untapped strength,
To rewrite the narrative and go to great lengths.

Embrace compassion, let kindness ignite,
Spread unity's flame with all oyour might,
For unity, like a beacon, shall lead the way,
Casting aside darkness, creating a brand-new day.

Through troubled streets and shadowed alleys,
Manifest peace with courage that rallies,
Believe that change is not a distant dream,
But a masterpiece waiting to redeem.
Philadelphia, we beseech thee now,

Liberate thy spirit, let us avow,
That violence has no place within our core,
We shall reclaim our city, forevermore.

Let's paint a portrait of harmony true,
Crafted by love, in each action we do,
Together we'll rise, oh youth so bright,Illuminate the path, banish the night.

For the power lies within your hands,
To sculpt a future where peace expands,
Philadelphia's heartbeat, forever changed, By the passion and love you've exchanged.

So, take this poem and let it reside,
Within your hearts, as you stride, Towards a city reborn, no longer in strife,
With violence vanquished, reclaiming life.

Now, let the echoes of hope resound,
For in unity, a brighter future is found,
Philadelphia's youth, your strength unfurled,
Together we'll transform the world.

My Dearest Rahmeek

Words cannot express the depth of sorrow and anguish that fills my heart as I pen this heartfelt letter to you. The pain is unbearable, the grief so overwhelming that it feels as though every breath I take is weighed down by a heaviness I cannot shake off. How could this happen? How could someone so dear, so cherished, be ripped away from us in such a senseless act of violence?

I still remember the day we first met, like it was yesterday. The moment our eyes locked, it was as if we had known each other for a lifetime. You brought so much joy and laughter into my life, and our friendship blossomed into something truly beautiful. We shared our dreams, our hopes, and our deepest fears. We were there for each other through thick and thin, supporting one another in every endeavor.

And now, my friend, you are gone, taken from this world in the most horrific way imaginable. I will never forget the day when tragedy struck and I found myself covered in your innocent blood. The sense of shock and helplessness that engulfed me in that moment still haunts my every waking thought. How could I have failed to

protect you?
But I want you to know, my dear friend that your memory lives on in my heart. Your infectious laughter, your unwavering strength, and your compassionate soul are etched into the very fabric of my being. The pain of losing you will never fully subside, but I will honor your memory by living my life with the same zest and passion that you possessed.

I will hold onto the cherished moments we shared, the late-night conversations filled with laughter, the adventures we embarked upon together, and the tears we shed in times of sorrow. Your loss has reminded me of the preciousness of life, of the fleeting beauty that can be shattered in an instant. I vow to make the most of every moment, to live a life that exemplifies the kind of person you were - loving, caring, and full of light.

Though you are no longer physically present, your spirit endures. Your love continues to guide me through the darkest of nights, and your memory will forever serve as a source of inspiration and strength. I will be the voice that fights for justice, the advocate for the lives torn apart by senseless violence, for your memory demands that justice prevails.

My dear friend, know that you will never be forgotten. Your legacy will live on through the lives you touched, the hearts you filled with love, and the memories we shared. In your honor, I will strive to be the best version of myself and to spread the kindness and compassion that you radiated effortlessly.

Rest in peace, my beloved friend. Your light will continue to shine brightly, reminding us all of the preciousness of life and the importance of cherishing those we hold dear. Until we meet again.

With eternal love and devotion,Paul aka Jundi

A Letter to Paul

Dear Paul,
I hope this letter finds you in good spirits, despite the challenges you may be facing at this moment. I understand that you are feeling depressed, overwhelmed, and even considering the unthinkable. Please know that Iam here for you, and I want to offer my support and guidance during this difficult time.

Firstly, I want you to remember that you are not alone in this struggle. Depression is an all-encompassing battle, but it does not define your worth or your potential for growth and happiness. Reach out to those around you - friends, family, or professionals - who can lend a listening ear and provide the necessary support. You do not have to go through this alone; there are people who care for you deeply and want to help you.
It is important to acknowledge that missing deadlines foryour goals can feel devastating, especially when it seemslike everyone around you is progressing effortlessly. However, remember that life is not a race, and setbacks are simply opportunities for growth and self-reflection. Take a step back and reassess your goals – are theymanageable? Are they aligned with

who you are and what you truly desire? Perhaps this momentary pausecan lead to a reevaluation of what truly matters to you, and allow you to refine your path towards a more fulfilling future.

During this challenging time, it is crucial to prioritize self-care and self-compassion. Be gentle with yourself, just as you would with a close friend. Engage in activities that bring you joy and provide a sense of calmness, such as spending time in nature, practicingmindfulness, or pursuing creative outlets. Cultivate a routine that nurtures your physical and mental well- being, incorporating exercise, nutritious meals, and quality sleep into your daily life. Taking care of your basic needs is paramount to rebuilding your emotional resilience.

Furthermore, consider seeking professional help from a therapist or counselor who can provide the necessary tools and techniques to navigate through this difficult period. They can offer you constructive guidance and equip you with coping strategies to manage your depression and suicidal thoughts. Remember, asking for help does not signal weakness; it reveals strength and a commitment to your own well-being.

Lastly, it is crucial to hold onto hope, even when it feels like everything is falling apart. Remember that life is an extraordinary journey with ups and downs, and your current struggles do not define who you are or what you are capable of achieving. You have a reservoir of strength and resilience within you, waiting to be tapped into. Believe in your own ability to overcome adversity and find solace in the fact that brighter days lie ahead. Please know that you are valued, loved, and deserving of a life filled with happiness and fulfillment. Reach out to those who care about you and let them help you through this difficult time. Remember, it is not the destinationbut the journey that truly matters.

With heartfelt support and belief in your strength.Love always,

Jundi

Entrepreneurship

In the realm of dreams, I tread,
An entrepreneur, forging ahead.
With a vision clear, a spirit unbowed,
I weave my path through the crowd.

Risk is my compass, courage my guide,
In the face of uncertainty, I stride.
An idea, a dream, a fervent desire,
Fuels my journey, and ignites my fire.

Lonely are the nights, tough are the days,
Yet, in my heart, a steadfast blaze.
For every failure, every fall, Strengthens my resolve,
above all.

Innovation is my craft, creation my art,
Every setback, a fresh start.
In the market's tumultuous sea,
I sail my venture, bold and free.

Through sleepless nights and endless toil,
I sow my dreams in challenging soil.
Yet, the fruits of labor, sweet and ripe,
Are worth every struggle, every gripe.

Every sunrise brings new hope,
With every sunset, I learn to cope.
Guided by passion, driven by grit,
In the entrepreneur's chair, I sit.

This journey of mine, arduous and long,
Shapes me, and makes me strong.
For I am an entrepreneur, brave and bright,
Chasing my dreams, with all my might.

The Feeling of Loneliness

In a world teeming with voices, I stand alone, Amongst the crowd, my sorrows are unknown. Surrounded by masks of joy and cheer,
Yet, does anyone see me? Does anyone hear?

Friends, they call themselves, their laughter loud, Yet behind their eyes, no sincerity is found.
Their smiles, they flash, their words, they spin,
But their hearts, are hollow, and their promises, thin.

Loved ones near yet so far away,
Lost in their worlds, in their own array. Preoccupied with life's unending race,
In their hurried pursuit, they forget my face.

Do you see me? I ask, my voice a mere whisper,
At the edge of their world, fading and crisper.
Do you hear me? I plead, my heart aching,
But my words, they get lost, in their constant making.

I trusted once, twice, thrice, and again,
In people, in love, in the comfort of a friend.
Yet each time, I was left with a scar,
A painful reminder of trust, gone too far.

I'm tired, so tired, my spirit is worn,
By loneliness, by deceit, by love, that's torn. But in this pain, a strength does reside,
A will to endure, a refusal to hide.

Yes, I am alone, but I am not lost,
My heart may be weary, but it knows the cost.
For in the silence, in the pain, in the quiet night,
I find myself, I find my light.

Building Blocks

Oh, my dear niece and nephews, gather close and listen well,
For I have a tale to tell, a message to impart,
I fervently swell.
In this journey we call life, there's a truth I want to share,
That you are allowed to stumble, it's okay, and you're allowed to care.

Life's path may seem uncertain, riddled with twists andturns,
But even when mistakes are made, remember how a phoenix yearns.
For from the ashes, they do rise, stronger than before,
And in every setback lies a chance to explore.

So dream big, my precious ones, never fear the unknown,
For within your very soul, courage is surely sown.
In chasing your aspirations, embrace the lessons learned,
For it's in those bittersweet moments that true wisdom is earned.

The road may sometimes get rough, obstacles may arise,
But know that with each battle, your spirit will surelyrise.
Believe in yourselves, my loves, hold steadfast to yourworth,
You possess the strength within you, a treasure of immeasurable girth.

I want to be an example, a guiding light in your way,

To show you it's okay to falter, to stumble, to lose yourway.
For the true test of character lies not in reaching thepeak,
But in how you rise again, the choice is yours to seek.

Discover your passions, pursue them without fear,
Because greatness lies within you, my darlings, it's sonear.

Do not be afraid of falling, of facing life's uncertain tides,
For it is when you rise from the depths that a warriorresides.

So, my nieces and nephews, embrace life's ebb and flow,
Know that mistakes are not failures, but a chance to grow.
You have the power within to be the best that you can be,
Now go forth and conquer, for your dreams await, you see.

With playful hearts and passionate souls, go forth withconfidence,
For you have the ability to overcome any circumstance.
In this life, my precious ones, make mistakes, learn, andrise,
And let your spirit soar, to reach the limitless skies.

Recipe for a Long-Lasting Love

Ingredients:
1 cup of commitment
2 cups of communication
3 3 cups oftrust
4 cups of respect
5 cups of laughter
6 cups of patience
7 cups of quality time
8 cups of understanding
9 cups offorgiveness
10 cups of affection

Instructions:

1. Preheat the oven of love to a warm and caring temperature.

2. In a large mixing bowl, combine commitment andcommunication. Stir well until fully blended.

3. Gradually add trust, one cup at a time. Mix thoroughlyto ensure all doubts and insecurities are eliminated.

4. Gently fold in respect, making sure to give each otherspace and valuing each other's opinions and choices.
Sprinkle laughter generously. This ingredient adds joy and happiness, creating a strong bond.

6. Slowly pour patience into the mix. Stir gently, allowing it to infuse with all the other ingredients.

7. Add quality time, ensuring you make time for each other, creating memories, and deepening the connection.

8. Carefully mix in understanding, making an effort to see things from your partner's perspective.

9. Slowly add forgiveness. This ingredient helps overcome misunderstandings and keeps grudges at bay.

10. Lastly, add affection. Pour it generously and make sure it's spread evenly, expressing love and appreciation for each other.

11. Bake in the oven of love for a lifetime, making necessary adjustments along the way.

Remember, this recipe requires constant effort, commitment, and love.
Enjoy the sweet taste of long-lasting love!

Loft Lounge

In Manayunk's vibrant streets, a gem shines bright,The
Loft Lounge, a haven for endless delight,
A hookah bar, restaurant, and lounge in one,
A place where stories are woven, and memories spun.

Step inside and surrender to the enchanting haze,
A symphony of flavors, as the hookah's smoke sways,
From fruity blends to exotic delights,
A sensory journey that ignites the nights.

The Loft Lounge, a sanctuary for the hungry souls,
A culinary haven where delectable dishes unfold, From
sizzling kebabs to savory bites,
A fusion of flavors that ignite appetites.

Tables adorned with laughter, glasses clinked in cheer,
Friends gather 'round, sharing tales far and near,
The ambiance was alive with the
music's sweet tune,
As melodies mingle, hearts begin
to swoon.

Artistic strokes grace the walls, a visual treat,
A gallery of expression where creativity meets,
The Loft Lounge, a canvas for talents to bloom,
A sanctuary for artists, a vibrant room.

Here, strangers become friends, and friendships grow,
A melting pot of cultures, a harmonious flow,
As conversations flow like the river's embrace,
Connections are forged, leaving no trace.

From dusk till dawn, the Loft Lounge's doors wide,
Welcoming all seekers of joy, side by side,
A tapestry of moments, hand in hand,
Creating memories that forever expand.

Oh, Loft Lounge, you're a beacon of pleasure,
A sanctuary where souls find their treasure,
In Manayunk's heart, you stand tall and proud,
A destination of flavors, where dreams are allowed.

So let us gather, in this haven of delight,
Where hookah, food, and laughter unite,
The Loft Lounge, a place where hearts find solace,
A haven of indulgence, a heavenly palace.

Mr D

To my mother's husband, a friend so dear,
Whose presence in our lives brings boundless cheer,
With gratitude in my heart, I now pen,
A poem of appreciation, time and again.

Through the ups and downs, you've always been there,
A pillar of strength, showing love and care,
You've stood by, my mother, a constant support,
Through every challenge that life may distort.

Not just a husband, but a friend sincere,
Whose wisdom and guidance I always revere,
Your words of encouragement, like ripples in a stream,
Guide me forward, fulfilling my dreams.

We may not always see eye to eye,
Yet, your patience and understanding never die,
In our differences, lessons we find,
The beauty of growth, together entwined.

And oh, the Eagles, our glorious team,
In the triumphs and losses, we jointly scream,
The joy we share as we watch them soar,
Our love of the game, forever we'll adore.

From laughter to tears, through thick and through thin,
You've proven time and again, we will always win,
For in your company, moments come alive,
Celebrating victories, as together we strive.

So here's to you, my mother's beloved,

A treasure in our lives, from stars above,
For being a friend, a source of light,
Guiding us through both day and night.

May our journey together forever thrive,
As a family bonded, always alive,
With gratitude overflowing, I extend my plea,
Thank you, dear stepfather, for being there for me.

Dear Philadelphia Police Department,

In a world where shadows weep,
Where injustice seeks no sleep,
Let our voices rise as one,
To challenge deeds that must be undone.

To the brave protectors in blue,
We humbly turn to speak to you,
In these words of empathy and plea,
To embrace a future that's truly free.

Like the open sky, let justice soar,
Where kindness triumphs evermore,
For hearts are fragile, colors diverse,
Let not fear be the driver, let it disperse.

For heroes in uniform, we believe,
With the power of change, we shall achieve,
A world where dreams don't shatter and break,
Where fairness and compassion awake.

In the depths of darkness, a glimmer of light,
Unveiling truths that can no longer be slight,
In unity, we must stand, hand in hand,
Where love and respect forever expand.

We beseech you, guardians of the law,
To heed this plea, to heed this call,
Seek the light within, your oath to uphold,
For every life matter, regardless of mold.

Embrace empathy's embrace, let it carry,
With the dignity of humanity's ferry,

For together we can rewrite the story,
Where justice reigns supreme in all its glory.

In this profound moment, let's embrace,
The power of change, the chance to erase,
The pain and suffering that divide,
And build a new, let justice abide.

From the depths of our souls, we implore,
To stop the violence, to heal and restore,
A world where color no longer dictates,
Where harmony prevails, love never abates.

Let history reflect our courage and zeal,

As unity becomes more than an ideal,
To protect and serve, with fairness and grace,
For every life, every creed, every race.

Inspire hearts to empathize,
Bridge the gaps, where prejudice lies,
For a future where we all stand tall,
United, equal, and answering love's call.

So, we entreat you, brave police,
Let compassion guide your every peace,
Together we can redefine the role,
And reclaim the essence of the human soul.
Jundi Allah

For My Mama

In a world of darkness, she's a shining light,
A warrior in battles, through every lonely night,
She bears an unmatched strength, a hero through andthrough,
My mom, my hero, her strength's a balm that soothes.

She's a trauma survivor, a soul that's been tested,
Yet she rises above, her heart never arrested,
With every challenge faced, she finds the courage to go,
My mom, my hero, a survivor in the throes.

Through tears and heartaches, she's stood tall,
overcoming shadows, and never letting them install,
Her spirit, resilient, shines like the morning sun,
My mom, my hero, a story of battles won.

She's a trauma survivor, a soul that's been tested,
Yet she rises above, her heart never arrested,
With every challenge faced, she finds the courage to go,My mom, my hero, a survivor in the throes.

Though scars may linger, etched upon her heart,
Strength radiates from her, a work of timeless art,
She's taught me to rise above, to never be afraid,
With her love as my guide, through any darkness, we'llwade.

She's a trauma survivor, a soul that's been tested,
Yet she rises above, her heart never arrested,
With every challenge faced, she finds the courage to go,
My mom, my hero, a survivor in the throes.

In this poem, is my gratitude so sincere,
For my mom, my hero, who's always been near,
Through thick and thin, together we will stride,
Forever grateful for her, my hero, my mom, and myguide.
I love you.

I am love

I am Love, both gentle and fierce,
The healing balm for wounds is diverse.
I am the whisper in the wind,
The unseen force that's always been.

I am the dawn's first gleaming ray,
The comfort at the end of the day.
I am the laughter, I am the tears,
The antidote to all your fears.

I am Love, in a mother's touch,
In a lover's gaze, that means so much.
I am the bond between friends so true,
The spark that makes the old feel new.

I am the silence in the night,
The courage that instills the fight.
I am the strength when hope seems gone,
The melody in every song.

I am Love, in a child's smile,
In the journey of every mile.
I am the peace in a world of strife,
The rhythm and pulse in every life.

I am the hand that holds you tight,
The beacon in the darkest night.
I am the faith when doubts arise,
The truth that counters every lie.

I am Love, both vast and wide,
An endless, ever-flowing tide.
In every heart, in every soul,
Making the wounded spirits whole.

So, when despair clouds your sun,
Remember, I am Love, we are one.
In every moment, in every shove,
Know this - I am, and will always be, Love.

Building Happiness

In the depths of your soul, where dreams hold sway,
I'll weave a verse to dissolve obstacles that lay.
With words as my weapon, I'll paint a dazzling scene,
A tempest of resilience, fierce and serene.

Oh, let this poem uproot the weeds of disdain,
Unleash a force that sets your spirit aflame.
Destroy every hindrance, every strand of strife,
As you embark on the quest for a joyous life.

I'll summon the sun's rays to pierce through the gray,
Illuminating paths in your chosen way.
With each line, a tempest shall gather its might,
Unfolding a power that conquers the night.

Together we'll march in a fearless endeavor,
As words morph into shields, our spirits shall sever,
The chains that bind, the doubt that holds tight,
Destroying all obstacles blocking your sight.

I'll summon the rivers to wash away doubt,
Unleash the winds to blow courage about.
For no mountain too vast, no valley too deep,
Can withstand the force of a soul daring to leap.

In every stanza, resilience shall surge,
With rhythm and rhyme like an unyielding urge.
We'll forge a path to traverse the unknown,
Dismantling fears, leaving none overthrown.

Through valleys of shadows, where hopes dimmed bydespair,
This poem shall rise, a phoenix in the air.
We'll shatter the glass ceiling of doubt and dismay,

Unleashing your happiness in a riotous display.

Let this poem be the anthem of your bliss,
A lighthouse in storms, a gentle, loving kiss.
With every word, may you find strength anew,
As you chase your dreams and make them come true.

So, let's embark now on this poem's sweet vow,
To demolish all barriers that hinder you now.
Inscribed in the lines, let your spirit ignite,
And may your pursuit of happiness shine so bright.

Untitled

In the heart of the industrial song,
Where the rhythm of creation is strong,
A desire is born, a passion takes flight,
To become a sheet metal apprentice, in the steel's moonlight.

Not for the gold, or the glimmer of fame,
But for the craft, the art in the frame,
It's not just metal, it's not just heat,
It's a symphony of hands, where skill and substance meet.

The furnace roars, the hammers strike,
In this labor, I find delight,
In the dance of fire and steel,
In the symphony of creation, I zealously kneel.

The raw power of metal, the whispering flame,
In every curve, every angle, I stake my claim,
To shape, to mold, to bend, to fold,
In the heart of the forge, where stories are told.

I yearn to learn the secrets it holds,
Of alchemy, in the shape of molds,
To craft from chaos, to create from raw,
In each piece, a part of me,
I flawlessly draw.

In the silence of the workshop,
I find my voice,In the choice of the craft,
I make my choice,

To be an apprentice, in the realm of steel,
In the dance of creation, I wish to kneel.

For each sheet of metal holds a tale,
Of resilience and strength, that never goes stale,
In every cut, every bend, every fold,
A new chapter of my journey is gently told.

So, here I stand, on the edge of a dream,
In the heart of the forge, where the anvils scream,
To be a sheet metal apprentice, in the dance of the fire,
In the symphony of creation, is my undying desire.

The Eulogy

Oh, alcohol, you were once my dear friend,
A companion in times of joy and despair,
But now it is time for our bond to end,
For a future without you, I must declare.

You came to me with promises untold,
A temporary refuge from life's strife,
But slowly, you took control and stole,
The dreams and ambitions of my life.

Into your arms, I willingly fell,
Seeking solace and a momentary high,
But the depths you took me, I cannot tell,
Leaving me broken, empty, and dry.

No more shall I partake in your poison,
No more shall I surrender to your hold,
With clarity and strength, I have chosen,
To walk away, my heart resolutely bold.

For the mornings of regret and despair,
Wake-up calls ring loudly in my head,
I want to be free from your toxic snare,
To embark on a new path, unafraid.

No more shall I sacrifice my well-being,
To drown my sorrows in your bitter embrace,
I choose sobriety and a life of meaning,
To let my spirit soar, to find my true place.

Farewell, alcohol, you're no longer wanted,
In my life, you have caused enough pain,
I bid you adieu, though it may be haunted,
With memories tarnished by your disdain.

From this day forth, my heart shall be unbound,
Released from the shackles that held me back,
I'll build a life where joy and peace are found,
And never again shall I traverse your track.

So, raise a glass, not filled with your deceiving lure,
But one of clarity, filled with hope and grace,
For I am free, I bid you an eternal adieu,
To forever break up, and find a better chase.

In passing

In a bustling street, where strangers meet,
A poem I craft for you is so kind and sweet.
If kindness is what you desire, just let me know,
I'll lend a hand, wherever you may go.

In this game of life, I'm rooting for you,
May victory, your path, forever pursue.
Through trials and triumphs,
I'll always be nearby,
To give you a listening ear, to chase away any fear.

So stranger, remember, you're not alone,
Together, in this journey, we have grown.
Let our paths collide, our souls intertwine,
For in this world, compassion is a precious sign.

A Note from the Author

I would like to personally thank you for purchasing my first book and taking the time to go on the journey with me on each page. Until next time, my dear friend.
Jundi

Please don't forget to support our scholarship at gofund.me/03d1698a

Made in the USA
Middletown, DE
20 March 2024

51667076R00050